# Kissing Nests

## Werner Lutz

*Translated from the German by*
*Marc Vincenz*

SPUYTEN DUYVIL

*New York City*

Publication of this volume is in part made possible by ProHelvetia, the Swiss Arts Council.

prohelvetia

A number of these translations were first published in *Asymptote Journal.*


Cover art: Werner Lutz, *Kissing Nests*
ISBN 978-1-881471-63-9

Library of Congress Cataloging-in-Publication Data

Lutz, Werner, 1930-
[Kussnester. English]
Kissing nests / Werner Lutz ;
translated from the German by Marc Vincenz.
p. cm.
Poems.
ISBN 978-1-881471-63-9
I. Vincenz, Marc. II. Title.
PT2672.U828K8713 2012
831'.914--dc23
2012025957

# Contents

*Kissing Nests*

Poems
read them once darkly
once lightly
read them with the eyes of midday
and read them
with the eyes of midnight

Imagine
there is peace within you
contented shrubbery
grows in your center
inhabited by sparrows
a tribe of cheeky
chirping sparrows

Daydreamed of this and that
showed myself in a better light
river trout exposed
on my table
so the whole thing becomes quicksilver

Yes I'll try
to read the letters
I never receive

to understand
why it's so monosyllabic
around me
without warm wishes
and without a "See you soon"

Within familiar noises
what just can't be true
lies hidden

Embers lie on the colors
shards of light crackle
and over everything
the magical eye
of the blazing circle burns

we will have to plant
thick impenetrable shadows
and dig deep echoing wells

Today the clouds hum
and the ones up north
somewhat deeper than usual

Left standing
in a bewildering yellow
left standing near the heart
with a wide vision
on the past

Let wind plant avenues
not gardens of prudence

It doesn't help but still
I have to dwell on futile things
how it might be how it would be

if the roots
of an ancient oak would grow
through the chambers of my heart
with their narcotic juices
their poison and their
wisdom of the evergreen

Waiting simply waiting
until
behind the rain-soaked scents
the gardens show themselves again

Look up
point up
what's up there is worth
pointing the index finger at

what normally sticks heavy and slimy
to shoe soles
floats cloudlessly today

Voices
foam-wrestling women
high priestesses of the tralali tralala
soloists of the ear-trombone

Aha
they surely arose
those sharp malicious tongues
directly from the street dirt
way up
in a cloud-crib weaned on cloud-humming

and even further up into the airless space
where all around regard
hindsight insight rule
and unchanging sunlight

Artful lies
hard tumbles
deep self-pity
silent times of waiting
are also familiar to me
as is the cooing pecking
simplicity of her pigeons

He had written poems
peach-colored ones too
he had written poems
within a blue haze
he had cheated with them
he had loved with them

Something buzzes
in the fabric of my coat
something sniggers
in the weave of my years

Startled
by a falling plantain leaf
I begin to realize
that I don't need
to worry myself anymore
about what was good
or what was pathetic

Would you listen
to those earthy laughs
look at them
those clay figures
always on the move
to new wonders

Can I say
the trees have become more tree-like
since yesterday
their wood woodier their leaves leafier

can I say
the folk have become more folksy
since yesterday
and the curios more curious than ever before

Facts
should be turned and rotated
between the fingers
in order to discover
if they still live
or have long perished

To attack
or just holding on
bracing oneself against
and to marvel at the power
of futility

a leafless time
earthy steps can be heard
in the freshly plowed fields
and on the verbs
the restrained luster
of oxidizing metal

Flying is easier
with empty hands

And here she is again
the desire to touch the untouched
to draw lines through the morning
out into open breezes
and the hand's pleasure
in feeling
the refreshing wind

Yes
it's the wrong moment
and yes
it's the wrong hand
that wants to touch me

A gloaming
that covers the hands
that covers faces
a gloaming
that makes us to things
to covered things

Time
to grab a bit of melancholy
to grant oneself
that big swig of Burgundy
to coax oblivion
into dance

Who feeds the evening
with red sunset
me
always just me

A hand waves flutters flickers
a stillness stares at me
with deep probing eyes

this thickly clad stillness
is my lover
and the coolness of evening
at the same time

To surprise oneself
in the wink of an eye
to visit oneself
unexpectedly whimsically

Hardly anyone
treads cautiously with himself
lies his hand
on the other hand
gives the warmth
and takes the warmth
of the one
with the other hand

To accept
what doesn't smell like soap
the blackness behind the colorful
the unveiled apathy
of morning

Tile-red afternoon
lead-heavy glazing
clay-dark hands

the light remains immovable
hangs in the trees
the light remains immovable
lies in the hands

the light feels like stone

The fresh scent
of freshly written lines
breezes through the morning

The yearning for white
unwritten paper
a reflecting upon itself
a slow heartbeat
poems
that only hesitantly open themselves
in the clumsy left hand

In spite of the piddling rain
in spite of the middling rain
I dare
to laugh
an inaudible laughter

Dribbling reports of humdrum
memory flowers made of wax

Hands
that web themselves in cocoons
daybutterflyhands nightmothhands

Country rain
that seeps all the way
into the cores of the ripening fruit

Nerves on edge
stomach-storm
an urge to cough
and at night the burning
geraniums in front of the window

Hand that rummages in colors
throws up a red
that catches a twittering

Hand that buries death
and tames night

Hand
that puts itself to one side
and forgets itself

Writing on
through the years is the thing
that makes me a second

Listening to the blooming
the never quite born
never quite awakened blooming

leave it
leave it off

don't listen to the music
the fragrance of the colors
perceived even in sleep

could be
that you dare to touch a single bloom
and then for always remain mute

Here spring is
a clear
light-sodden sin
cradled
by the hills
and pacified by us

I always sleep badly in March
lie under silk paper
and the perfume of distant foreign yearning
lets me breathe quicker

the hours turn
their seductive rounds
and on these nights what I think
is similar to the buds in March

too early too early
too reckless to be viable

Reeling thoughts are burgundy colors
burgundy reeling is thought colors

I wanted to write
to tell you I miss you
but my left hand
already sleeps
and my right hand
drank too much wine

what should I do

very early tomorrow
I want to gather words for you
pebblewords
that can take it on
with any opal

He who loves dares losing
leaves the colors burning

Tonight I want to sleep
in a deep ultramarine
from the other side of oceans

tonight I want to believe
you lie next to me
and your breaths
accompany my breaths
as mine accompany yours
it doesn't matter where

Desires
shout and yell
come on
let's go
to Rotterdam
and throw themselves
into the Rhine

Kissing nests well hidden
in the evening

and along the river
chestnut tree after chestnut tree
strolling branch in branch
arm in arm

like couples that tolerate each other
after all these long years

Don't breathe a word
I beg of you
your words will only bring
the winter into the house

Later tell me later
when the evening branches off

and that derisive glittering laughter
will be echoed in the leaves of the pear tree
that stands fastidiously drawn
in the counterlight

think about the fragility of words

Oh yes
verse is bric-a-brac
ding-dung
and not worth the words

Ointment dribbles from the chamomile
and a snail track shimmers

dark giant pupils
suck in the leftover light
of day

rosequartzlove
is finally still
the poems listen in on themselves

A sun-warmed rustle
tries to kiss the midday stillness

I wish
never to forget
not your eyes still full of sleep
not your lashes
that kiss butterfly kisses
and the tickling on the skin
until a pebble-round laughter
rolls through the dawn
and we miss the morning
because of this
and no other reason

I can only vaguely
describe it
that trembling gentle pink
in the light green moment

Fleeting eyes leafy whispers
deliberations
on the swinging trapeze

remaining concealed forever
the first shy togethernesses
chirping in the high summer grass

and unforgotten
the inaudible screaming fragrances
light-headed and wanton
in the lilac bush cut down long ago

He's thirsty
that love-thirsty
bird within me
who hops from rib
to rib
as if they were branches

It can't be that impossible
with me

look
seldom seen bird species
have returned
to nest
in the lines of my poems

Can you tell me
how a yes
tastes on the tongue

White whitewashed hours
between white whitewashed walls

and still something is underfoot

a dust-dancing dust-mote
that lives off sunrays

impermanent love
disastrously impetuous
unspeakably short

It's even possible
to live in the space between

Once in summer
when green tendernesses
slept in half shadows

once in autumn
when the pear trees deepened themselves
into their own embers

once in winter
when snow gusts
blanketed the standstill

once in spring
a goodbye waved
from the roadside

something black was blooming
on the blackbriar bush

A thoroughly sun-warmed person
sun-warmed even now in October
not a fugitive not an exile
not a burden on this day thanks to you

I'm taking this landscape with me
to show her to you
her swinging lines
that remind me of you

those bright strips of foehn cloud
as if one could hear your laughter
in the glowing autumn
of the alder leaves

Careful
laughing about obscurities
even scoffing them
can be perilous

Night
to keep secrets

night to not be cheated on
by day

no night isn't lightless
not without chlorophyll

and not without the whispers of dreams
that have always been sleepless

Moss covered
clouds drive into evening
an evening almost made
for asking
deaf-mute things
are you alright

are you alright

In this case good advice is expensive
the evening mocks
from behind me
there are heads
which no hat fits

It could be
that still-standing times
unconscious times do exist
a dominion the moon holds
over broad daylight

The farewell came
too early today
too early this quiet whirring darkness

let me say it anyway

I stand outside
far outside of myself
surrounded by graves

that I'm always impelled to adorn

I write these lines blindly
write them eavesdropping
on nocturnal paper

Maybe grey is
the most reliable color
more a condition
than a thing of light
similar to a sickness
one gradually
begins to endure

Dance-mobs of mosquitoes
practice the twirl for no apparent reason

Even though I'm feverish I'm cold
my attempts to become simple
have failed in their complexity

not for the first time
the forest also rambles
over the wrong path
in the west a red evening glow
like a richly branched masterpiece of roots

What on earth is the evening up to
up there
in the rainclouds of the blessed

Walking towards sleep
stumbling towards dreams
already missing the rays
missing the warmth

and a cool little breeze
that rested
too long
in a tree's shadow
goes on his way

Who would be so mad
as to dish out insurgencies
in the room of dreams

Evening hours
their outlines their oval shapes
their teardrop forms

how finely everything is divided
into small and even smaller
glimpses in moments
thoughts in thought-dust

It makes no sense
in autumn rain
to also cry
about the spilt summer

Distant September
distant flocks of birds

a dusty
lipless grin

too late in the year
too uncertain

to hear the slapping of waves
at the riverbank

words lightly bantered
a playful timelessness

Foehn clouds bind
swifts bind
simply bind
what cannot be bound

Like a curse
this evening arrives
over the Rhine

the towers sink
in the muddy light

the sandstone towers
winding staircase towers
the towers
of the futile prayers

the cottonwood on the shore
woven with cobwebs
made of pleading
begging sounds

the lips taste
of a foreign voice

Foamy spattering laughter
and dancing lights from the shore
between the serious words of the night
line upon line
a flowing poem
written in the riverwater
by an old poet

Enchanting is the day
that knows no calendar

Revered distance

your spacey opinion
is also my opinion
and I greet you
in everlasting love
over the hills
as far as the valleys

and remain always
yours
Werner Lutz

**Werner Lutz** was born in Wolfhalden, Switzerland in 1930, and is considered to be one of Switzerland's foremost living lyric poets. He has been awarded numerous prizes for his work, including the Basel Lyric Prize (2010) and the city of Basel's Literary Prize (1996). He has published over eight collections of poetry and short fiction and currently lives in Basel, where he works as a poet, artist and graphic designer. This is his first full collection published in English.

**Marc Vincenz** is Swiss-British and was born in Hong Kong. His most recent books include *The Propaganda Factory, or Speaking of Trees* (Argotist, 2011) and *Pull of the Gravitons* (Right Hand Pointing, 2012). His translation of Swiss poet Erika Burkart's collection, *Secret Letter,* is forthcoming from Cervena Barva Press (2013). He currently lives in Iceland where he works as a journalist, poet, translator, editor and book designer. Recent and forthcoming publications include *Guernica*, *Exquisite Corpse*, *The Potomac*, *Spillway Review*, *Poetry Salzburg Review*, *elimae*, *MiPOesias* and *Stirring*. He is presently working on a verse novel, *Leaving Wolf Mountain*, and translating the works of Werner Lutz, Ernst Halter and Jon Kalmann Stefansson. Marc is Editor-in-Chief of MadHat Press and *Mad Hatters' Review*. In 2011, he was nominated four times for the Pushcart Prize.

## Spuyten Duyvil

*Meeting Eyes Bindery*

*Triton*

*Lithic Scatter*

***8th Avenue*** Stefan Brecht

***A Day and a Night at the Baths*** Michael Rumaker

***Acts of Levitation*** Laynie Browne

***Alien Matter*** Regina Derieva

***Anarchy*** Mark Scroggins

***Apo/Calypso*** Gordon Osing

***Apples of the Earth*** Dina Elenbogen

***Approximating Diapason*** hastain & thilleman

***Arc: Cleavage of Ghosts*** Noam Mor

***The Arsenic Lobster*** Peter Grandbois

***Ashes Rain Down*** William Luvaas

***Auntie Varvara's Clients*** Stelian Tanase

***Balkan Roulette*** Drazan Gunjaca

***The Banks of Hunger and Hardship*** J. Hunter Patterson

***La Belle Dame*** Gordon Osing & Tom Carlson

***Bird on the Wing*** Juana Culhane

***Black Lace*** Barbara Henning

***Black Mountain Days*** Michael Rumaker

***Blueprints For a Genocide*** Rob Cook

***Both Sides of the Niger*** Andrew Kaufman

***Breathing Free*** (ed.) Vyt Bakaitis

***Burial Ship*** Nikki Stiller

***Butterflies*** Brane Mozetic

***By The Time You Finish This Book You Might Be Dead*** Aaron Zimmerman

***Cadences*** j/j hastain

***Captivity Narratives*** Richard Blevins

***Celestial Monster*** Juana Culhane

***Cephalonical Sketches*** t thilleman

***Cleopatra Haunts the Hudson*** Sarah White

***Cloud Fire*** Katherine Hastings

***Columns: Track 2*** Norman Finkelstein

***Consciousness Suite*** David Landrey

***The Conviction & Subsequent Life of Savior Neck*** Christian TeBordo

***Conviction's Net of Branches*** Michael Heller

***The Corybantes*** Tod Thilleman

***Crossing Borders*** Kowit & Silverberg

***Day Book of a Virtual Poet*** Robert Creeley

***Daylight to Dirty Work*** Tod Thilleman

***The Desire Notebooks*** John High

***Detective Sentences*** Barbara Henning

***Diary of a Clone*** Saviana Stanescu

***Diffidence*** Jean Harris

***Donna Cameron*** Donna Cameron

***Don't Kill Anyone, I Love You*** Gojmir Polajnar

***Dray-Khmara as a Poet*** Oxana Asher

***Egghead to Underhoof*** Tod Thilleman

***Eroticizing the Nation*** Leverett T. Smith, Jr.

***The Evil Queen*** Benjamin Perez

***Exiled From the Womb*** Adrian Sangeorzan

***Extreme Positions*** Stephen Bett

***The Farce*** Carmen Firan

***Fission Among The Fanatics*** Tom Bradley

***The Flame Charts*** Paul Oppenheimer

***Flying in Water*** Barbara Tomash

***Form*** Martin Nakell

***Gesture Through Time*** Elizabeth Block

***Ghosts!*** Martine Bellen

***Giraffes in Hiding*** Carol Novack

***Gnostic Frequencies*** Patrick Pritchett

***God's Whisper*** Dennis Barone

***Gowanus Canal, Hans Knudsen*** Tod Thilleman

***Half-Girl*** Stephanie Dickinson

***Hidden Death, Hidden Escape*** Liviu Georgescu

***Houndstooth*** David Wirthlin

***Identity*** Basil King

***In Times of Danger*** Paul Oppenheimer

***Incretion*** Brian Strang

***Inferno*** Carmen Firan

***Infinity Subsections*** Mark DuCharme

***Insouciance*** Thomas Phillips

***Inverted Curvatures*** Francis Raven

***The Ivory Hour*** Laynie Browne

***Jackpot*** Tsipi Keller

***The Jazzer & The Loitering Lady*** Gordon Osing

***Kissing Nests*** Werner Lutz, trans. by Marc Vincenz

***Knowledge*** Michael Heller

***Lady V.*** D.R. Popa

***Last Supper of the Senses*** Dean Kostos

***A Lesser Day*** Andrea Scrima

***Let's Talk About Death*** M. Maurice Abitbol

***Light House*** Brian Lucas

***Light Years: Multimedia in the East Village, 1960-1966*** (ed.) Carol Bergé

***Little Book of Days*** Nona Caspers

***Little Tales of Family & War*** Martha King

***Long Fall: Essays and Texts*** Andrey Gritsman

***Lunacies*** Ruxandra Cesereanu

***Lust Series*** Stephanie Dickinson

***Lyrical Interference*** Norman Finkelstein

***Maine Book*** Joe Cardarelli (ed.) Anselm Hollo

***MannhatteN*** Sarah Rosenthal

***Mating In Captivity*** Nava Renek

***Meanwhile*** Gordon Osing

***Medieval Ohio*** Richard Blevins

***Memory's Wake*** Derek Owens

***Mermaid's Purse*** Laynie Browne

***Miming Mink*** j/j hastain

***Mobility Lounge*** David Lincoln

***Modern Adventures*** Bill Evans

***The Moscoviad*** Yuri Andrukhovych

***Multifesto: A Henri d'Mescan Reader*** Davis Schneiderman

***My Last Century*** Joanna Sit

***The New Beautiful Tendons*** Jeffery Beam

***No Perfect Words*** Nava Renek

***No Wrong Notes*** Norman Weinstein

***North & South*** Martha King

***Notes of a Nude Model*** Harriet Sohmers Zwerling

***Of All The Corners To Forget*** Gian Lombardo

***Onönyxa & Therseyn*** T Thilleman

***The Opening Day*** Richard Blevins

***Our Father*** M.G. Stephens

***Over the Lifeline*** Adrian Sangeorzan

***Pagan Days*** Michael Rumaker

***Part of The Design*** Laura E. Wright

***Pieces for Small Orchestra & other fictions*** Norman Lock

***A Place in the Sun*** Lewis Warsh

***The Poet : Pencil Portraits*** Basil King

***Political Ecosystems*** J.P. Harpignies

***Powers: Track 3*** Norman Finkelstein

***The Prison Notebooks of Alan Krieger (Terrorist)*** Marc Estrin

***Prurient Anarchic Omnibus*** j/j hastain

***Retelling*** Tsipi Keller

***Rivering*** Dean Kostos

***Root-Cellar to Riverine*** Tod Thilleman

***The Roots of Human Sexuality*** M. Maurice Abitbol

***Saigon and other poems*** Jack Walters

***A Sardine on Vacation*** Robert Castle

***Savoir Fear*** Charles Borkhuis

***Secret of White*** Barbara Tomash

***Seduction*** Lynda Schor

***See What You Think*** David Rosenberg

***Settlement*** Martin Nakell

***Sex and the Senior City*** M. Maurice Abitbol

***Sketches in Norse & Forra*** t thilleman

***Sketches Tzitzimime*** t thilleman

***Slaughtering the Buddha*** Gordon Osing

***The Snail's Song*** Alta Ifland

***SOS: Song of Songs of Solomon*** j/j hastain

***The Spark Singer*** Jade Sylvan

***Spiritland*** Nava Renek

***Strange Evolutionary Flowers*** Lizbeth Rymland

***Suddenly Today We Can Dream*** Rutha Rosen

***The Sudden Death of...*** Serge Gavronsky

***The Takeaway Bin*** Toni Mirosevich

***The Tattered Lion*** Juana Culhane

***Tautological Eye*** Martin Nakell

***Ted's Favorite Skirt*** Lewis Warsh

***Theater of Skin*** Gordon Osing & Tom Carlson

***Things That Never Happened*** Gordon Osing

***Thread*** Vasyl Makhno

***Three Mouths*** Tod Thilleman

***Three Sea Monsters*** Tod Thilleman

***Track*** Norman Finkelstein

***Transitory*** Jane Augustine

***Transparencies Lifted From Noon*** Chris Glomski

***Triple Crown Sonnets*** Jeffrey Cyphers Wright

***Tsim-tsum*** Marc Estrin

***Vienna ØØ*** Eugene K. Garber

***Uncensored Songs for Sam Abrams*** (ed.) John Roche

***Up Fish Creek Road*** David Matlin

***Warp Spasm*** Basil King

***Watchfulness*** Peter O'Leary

***Watch The Doors As They Close*** Karen Lillis

***Walking After Midnight*** Bill Kushner

***West of West End*** Peter Freund

***When the Gods Come Home to Roost*** Marc Estrin

***Whirligig*** Christopher Salerno

***White, Christian*** Christopher Stoddard

***Winter Letters*** Vasyl Makhno

***Within the Space Between*** Stacy Cartledge

***A World of Nothing But Nations*** Tod Thilleman

***A World of Nothing But Self-Infliction*** Tod Thilleman

***Wreckage of Reason*** (ed.) Nava Renek

***Xian Dyad*** Jason Price Everett

***The Yellow House*** Robin Behn

***You, Me, and the Insects*** Barbara Henning